RACE FOR YOUR LIFE!

24 HOURS OF LE MANS

BY KATE MIKOLEY

Gareth Stevens PUBLISHING

HOT TOPICS

Please visit our website, www.garethstevens.com. For a free color catalog of all our high-quality books, call toll free 1-800-542-2595 or fax 1-877-542-2596.

Library of Congress Cataloging-in-Publication Data

Names: Mikoley, Kate, author.
Title: 24 hours of Le Mans / Kate Mikoley.
Other titles: Twenty-four hours of Le Mans
Description: New York : Gareth Stevens Publishing, 2021. | Series: Race for your life! | Includes index.
Identifiers: LCCN 2020005102 | ISBN 9781538258965 (library binding) | ISBN 9781538258941 (paperback) | ISBN 9781538258958 (6 pack) | ISBN 9781538258972 (ebook)
Subjects: LCSH: 24 Heures du Mans (Automobile race)–Juvenile literature.
Classification: LCC GV1034.48.L4 M55 2021 | DDC 796.720944–dc23
LC record available at https://lccn.loc.gov/2020005102

First Edition

Published in 2021 by
Gareth Stevens Publishing
111 East 14th Street, Suite 349
New York, NY 10003

Designer: Laura Bowen
Editor: Kate Mikoley

Photo credits: Cover, pp. 1–32 (texture) Chatham172/Shutterstock.com; Cover, pp. 1 (car), 5, 29 (top) FRED TANNEAU/Contributor/AFP/Getty Images; pp. 7, 13, 17, 21, 25 Gerlach Delissen - Corbis/Contributor/Corbis Sport/Getty Images; p. 9 Martyn Goddard/The Image Bank Unreleased/Getty Images; p. 11 Gatroe/Wikimedia Commons; p. 15 Brian Cleary / Contributor/Getty Images Europe/Getty Images; pp. 19 (bottom), 27 James Moy Photography/Contributor/Getty Images Sports/Getty Images; pp. 19 (top), 23 JEAN-FRANCOIS MONIER/Contributor/AFP/Getty Images; p. 29 (winning team) JEAN-SEBASTIEN EVRARD/Stringer/AFP/Getty Images.

Printed in the United States of America

CPSIA compliance information: Batch #CS20GS: For further information contact Gareth Stevens, New York, New York at 1-800-542-2595.

CONTENTS

HITTING THE ROAD

Have you ever taken a long car trip? Just sitting in a car for a long time can get tiring. But some drivers love to spend hours behind the wheel of a race car. For them, the 24 Hours of Le Mans is the best race.

FEARLESS FACTS

The 24 Hours of Le Mans, often just called Le Mans, is one of the most well-known automobile, or car, races in the world.

You may have seen a car race before, but probably not one like the 24 Hours of Le Mans. Unlike other races, the cars at Le Mans aren't driving to reach a certain **distance**. They're racing to see which car can travel farthest in 24 hours!

FEARLESS FACTS

In many races, cars go around a track a certain number of times and the first finisher wins. At Le Mans, the cars just keep going until time's up. The winner is the car that drove the farthest!

RACE HISTORY

The first 24 Hours of Le Mans race was held in 1923. The race has been held almost every year since then. It takes place near the city of Le Mans, France, at the Sarthe road-racing circuit.

FEARLESS FACTS

The circuit is the course, or path, of the race. Part of the Le Mans course is a racetrack. Another part is on public roads.

At first, the 24 Hours of Le Mans was called Grand Prix de Vitesse et d'Endurance. This is French for Grand Prix of Speed and **Endurance**. Grand prix is a term commonly used for an **international** car race.

FIRST 24 HOURS OF LE MANS, 1923

FEARLESS FACTS

In its early days, the race was used as a way for car companies to show how strong the cars they made were.

RIGHT ON TRACK

The racecourse is a **loop** of about 8.5 miles (13.7 km). Drivers go around the course as many times as they can over the 24-hour race. The course has curves and turns, but drivers are at full speed about 85 percent of the time.

FEARLESS FACTS

Drivers still take turns fast, but they must be careful not to lose control of the car. This takes a lot of skill—and a special car!

TOP SPEED

Drivers commonly reach top speeds on straight parts of the course. One famous stretch is called the Mulsanne Straight. It's about 3.7 miles (6 km) of mostly straight road. Cars have reached over 250 miles (402 km) per hour here.

FEARLESS FACTS

A set of tight turns, called chicanes, have been added to the Mulsanne Straight to keep cars from going too fast. Still, cars commonly go faster than 200 miles (322 km) per hour.

TEAM TIME

Everyone needs rest. Having one person drive 24 hours straight would be very unsafe. That's why drivers in Le Mans are on teams made up of three drivers. Over the whole race, no driver can drive for more than 14 hours.

FEARLESS FACTS

Teams change drivers at the same time they stop for gas and have the tires changed. These periods are called pit stops.

Split up evenly, each driver would be behind the wheel for 8 hours, but teams don't have to split the driving equally. Each driver must drive between 6 and 14 hours. Driving **shifts** are often between 90 minutes and a few hours.

FEARLESS FACTS

Drivers can't drive for more than four hours within any six-hour period of time.

Having a team allows each driver some time to rest, eat, and make sure they're **alert** when they get back behind the wheel. Drivers don't get much sleep during the 24 hours of the race, but may take a quick nap between driving shifts.

FEARLESS FACTS

There's more to a team than drivers. The crew is important too! These are the people who change tires, fill the car with gas, and make other **repairs**.

THE CARS

It takes a special kind of car to race for 24 hours while reaching speeds over 200 miles (322 km) per hour. The cars in the race are known as sports cars. There are four different classes of cars racing at the same time.

FEARLESS FACTS

Cars on the course are commonly made by well-known companies, like Porsche, Ford, Toyota, and Mercedes-Benz.

The best two classes of cars in the race are the Le Mans **Prototype** 1 (LMP1) and Le Mans Prototype 2 (LMP2). These cars are built to race and cost a lot of money. LMP1s are the fastest cars in the race.

FEARLESS FACTS

Many cars in Le Mans are hybrids. This means they have both gas and electric **engines**.

The other two classes are grand touring cars. These look a bit like sports cars you might see on the street, but they're built in a special way to be fast and great for racing. They're faster than common cars, but not as fast as the LMP cars.

FEARLESS FACTS

One of the grand touring classes is for professionals, or people who race as a job. The other is for amateurs, or people who race as a hobby, not as a job.

RACE TO THE END

Every year in June, hundreds of thousands of fans go to watch the 24 Hours of Le Mans. Unlike other racing events, they can't be sure how far they'll see the cars race. Commonly, winners travel more than 3,100 miles (4,990 km)!

FEARLESS FACTS

To win at Le Mans, a team must work together. Winning teams need to have a great car, as well as great drivers.

SAFETY TIPS

- SLOW DOWN BELOW 37 MILES (60 KM) PER HOUR BEFORE COMING IN FOR A PIT STOP
- TURN OFF THE ENGINE BEFORE THE CREW STARTS WORKING ON THE CAR
- WATCH FOR OTHER CARS AND CRASHES ON THE COURSE
- FOLLOW SIGNS TELLING YOU TO SLOW DOWN
- WEAR SAFETY GEAR INCLUDING A HELMET
- USE BREAKS TO REST, EAT, AND DRINK WATER

FOR MORE INFORMATION

BOOKS

Kingston, Seth. *The History of Corvettes.* New York, NY: PowerKids Press, 2019.

Levit, Joe. *Motorsports Trivia: What You Never Knew About Car Racing, Monster Truck Events, and More Motor Mania.* North Mankato, MN: Edge Books, 2019.

WEBSITES

24 Hours of Le Mans
us.france.fr/en/loire-valley/article/24-hours-mans-0
Read more about this exciting event here.

Race Cars
www.dkfindout.com/us/transportation/history-cars/race-cars/
Find out all about race cars on this interactive page.

GLOSSARY

alert: able to think clearly and pay attention to things

distance: the amount of space traveled

endurance: the power to do something hard for a long time

engine: a machine that makes power

international: involving two or more countries

loop: a curved shape made when something bends around so that it comes back in contact with itself

prototype: the first model on which later models are based

repair: a fix made on something

shift: a period of time in which a person is working

INDEX